Faith like Flamingos

The Christian Business Guide to Walking Out Your Faith in Bold Color!

Katie Hepner

#FaithLikeFlamingos

PRAISE FOR *Faith Like Flamingos*

"With the creativity of an artist and the business acumen of a seasoned pro, Katie has written an encouraging book for entrepreneurs that is both practical and heartwarming. A big high-five to you Katie for a great book! And my highest recommendation of *Faith Like Flamingos* for all those who want to walk by faith in the marketplace."

Matt Tommey, Host
The Thriving Christian Artist Podcast
MattTommeyMentoring.com

"In Katie's new book, *Faith Like Flamingos*, you will find many ways to accomplish your purpose in life. There is no need to ever slump over with embarrassment, she teaches you how to stand tall embracing your uniqueness while never compromising your values".

Aaron Walker, Founder/President
View From The Top
ViewFromTheTop.com

"For too long Christians have been told to blend in, stay in the background and not raise a ruckus which is in opposition to the early church who were "loud and proud" about what truly mattered. They stood out, charged in front, and boldly proclaimed their faith. Today's Christian business owners should do the same. Katie will show you how. She is such a breath of fresh air in a stagnant world. Read *Faith Like Flamingos* carefully, absorb its message, and take action on what you are called to do."

Matt McWilliams, Founder
MattMcWilliams.com

"*Faith Like Flamingos* is a surprising flower of uniqueness in a desert of mediocrity. A whimsical work of art that delivers a serious message. The good news: you can be your amazing, one-of-a-kind self, stand out from the crowd, refuse to compromise your values ... and STILL succeed wildly. This book is your guide."

Ray Edwards, Founder
RayEdwards.com

"*Faith Like Flamingos* a delightful and much-needed read. For everyone, but especially women. Totally touched my heart for sure! Just the right length to digest and be able to contemplate throughout the day. Katie's heart, relatable storytelling and ability to pull in scripture and bring the living Word in is a true and blessed gift. Absolutely love this book."

Brenda Mason, Best-Selling Author
The 31-Day Guide to Create Your Clutter Free Home Oasis
SmallerLivingHugeLife.com

"If you have not read this, you must! I enjoyed reading it so much. It helped me focus my goals and reset my business vision to align with my faith. This is like no other business book out there."

Jennifer Anne Elia, Founder
JenniferAnneElia.com

"Faith Like Flamingos is a colorful, practical, and encouraging book to help Christian entrepreneurs be exactly who God has called them to be in their business. Katie has done an excellent job infusing her gift of storytelling, biblical wisdom, and business experience into a beautiful work of encouragement for Christian business owners."

Mike & Carlie Kercheval, Founders
Christian Marriage Adventures™
ChristianMarriageAdventures.com

"Katie, the way you draw connections between the beauty of one of God's Creations to another (us!) is powerful and oh so encouraging. We are all so different and I feel like this book is a celebration of that!"

Kelly McCausey
MomWebs.com

"I'm a busy homeschooling, work-at-home woman. I need powerful, biblical encouragement but I often don't have more than 10-15 minutes to read for business growth. *Faith Like Flamingos* is a power-packed book that gives me the best of both: encouragement, correction (in my thinking), business tips, and it's a quick daily read. Highly recommend it."

Danielle Tate, Founder
15MinuteMoneyManager.com

"How unique is the flamingo which shows me how unique my story is too! *Faith Like Flamingos* has challenged me to find stories from my childhood and adult life I can also use as teaching illustrations in my own writing."

Judith Kowles, Founder
HisUnmeasuredGrace.com

"Owning a business as a Christian can be a daunting experience. Not knowing when to be bold and when to be meek is such a struggle. In Faith Like Flamingos, Katie reaches the heart of the entrepreneur and reassures you that it's okay to embrace the gifts God has given you and share them with the world. It's okay to be exuberant and full of life, while pursuing your passion. This book should be on every business owner's "must read" list."

Stephanie Eidson, Founder
HomeschoolBlogging.com, TheMultitaskinMom.com

"I love this book. Faith Like Flamingos is so encouraging."

Teresa Morgan, Founder
BiblicalHospitality.com

"*Faith Like Flamingos* is a gem of a book! A multi - faceted diamond in the rough. Analogies stick with you. The writing is excellent, thought-provoking, and the message needed. The book was an easy read, but packed with help and meaning. Besides the spiritual and business teaching, it taught me so much about flamingos, too! I'll never look at a flamingo the same way again. Thank you for this. I love this book!"

Wendy Gunn, Founder
YourHomeForGod.com

"After a rough few months *Faith Like Flamingos* reminded me that I have no one but God to please. The only way to be successful in business and it is in following God's plan for me, which will not be like anyone else's. Tying the lessons into fun facts about the flamingo clarified them so that I was able to see where to correct my thinking. Congratulations on a truly great book. This is definitely needed as a source of Christian inspiration in a world so full of secular self-help books."

Bekah Morel, Founder, *MasonalaMaison.com*

#FaithLikeFlamingos

Faith Like Flamingos

The Christian Business Guide
to Walking Out Your Faith in Bold Color!
by Katie Hornor

Faith Like Flamingos © 2020 Katie Hornor

KatieHornor.com FelizPreneur LLC All rights reserved.

ISBN-13: 978-1-7346046-0-3

Original cover art © 2019 by Karina Hornor
Interior art purchased at Depositphoto. All art used by permission. All rights reserved.

Unless otherwise noted all Scripture quotations are from the *Holy Bible*, King James Version (KJV).

No part of this book may be reproduced in any form or by any electronic or mechanical means including information storage and retrieval systems, without permission in writing from the author. The only exception is by a reviewer, who may quote short excerpts in a review.

First Edition: 2020, printed in the USA.

#FaithLikeFlamingos

Get the *Bible Study* guide for individuals & groups, or the *Faith Like Flamingos Journal* at FaithLikeFlamingos.com

CLAIM YOUR FREE AUDIO BOOK!

Forward the purchase receipt of this book to FLF@katiehornor.com to get the audio book FREE!

Dedication:

To each of my Mastermind Members.
You are my Flamboyance. I am beyond blessed to
lead and learn from such a loyal community.

About the Author

Katie Hornor is a popular Christian author, women's business coach, mentor and international keynote speaker.

After leaving all for a ministry opportunity overseas only to have it pulled out from under them, Tap & Katie Hornor built a business and a movement in their second language among in the fastest growing market demographic in the world.

They created the only literature-based homeschool curriculum that exists in the Spanish language, and the first in history online summit for Spanish speaking home educators, so that Hispanic families around the world no longer suffer for lack of resources. They can experience the advantage of a personalized education and a better future for their children.

In addition to the Prek- 6th grade curriculum at Lemonhass.com, Katie has created 24 online courses, over 50 self-published books (including 5 best-sellers) and teaches her business clients to do the same so that they too can change the future for their clients. Katie's Lifestyle Business Podcast, ForYourSuccessPodcast.com has had such guests as John Lee Dumas, Aaron Walker, and Rachel Martin.

Her articles have been published in various places both on and offline including: The Huffington Post, Social Media Examiner Blog, and Homeschooling Today Magazine.

She has been a featured speaker at FinCon Expo, The Florida Parent Educator's Association Annual Conventions, SHIFTcon, and Social Media Week Lima, among others, and hosts her own semi-annual retreats for women business owners @BlogWellRetreats.

Born in Binghamton, NY, in 1979, Katie currently coaches Christian women in business from her home abroad in Campeche, Mexico, where she lives with her husband, managing their local coffee shop and homeschool ministry, and home educating their five children.

Invite Katie to speak at your next event by visiting KatieHornor.com

IG: @KatieHornor @BlogWellRetreats
T: @Katie_Hornor
P: @KatieHornor
LinkedIn: /KatieHornor
Podcast: KatieHornor.com/podcast

Women in Business Membership: TheBlogConnection.com
Retreats for Business Women of Faith: BlogWellRetreats.com
Women's Higher-Level Business Mastermind: QueensMastermind.com
Course Creation: BloggingSuccessfully.com/courses
Coaching: BloggingSuccessfully.com/coaching

Get the *Faith Like Flamingos Bible Study* guide and companion resources at FaithLikeFlamingos.com

Contents:

About the Author

Forword

Introduction

1. Pink Blooded Birds
2. You Are What You Eat
3. Pink and Not Sorry
4. Ugly Feature or Super Power?
5. Perfectly Awkward
6. You're Not Extinct Yet
7. Lead, Pinky!
8. Do the Mating Dance
9. A Single Focus
10. Pinker Than You
11. The Flamboyance Life
12. A Pink Ballet
13. Your Goose Honk
14. Delight In the Mud
15. Nourishment From a Different Perspective

16. Work Your Gland
17. I'm Molting!
18. What Black Feathers?
19. Standing On One Leg
20. When Do You sleep?
21. That's Using Your Legs!
22. Migrate Regularly
23. Pink Weather Ahead
24. Pink Forever
25. Don't Fear the Plastic

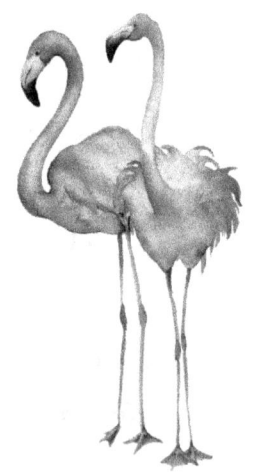

Forward:

The day had arrived that most business owners dread, but cannot avoid. It was picture day.

Photos for a business owner, whether brick and mortar or an online business, are crucial to the image you portray to your potential customers and community.

Pictures are more than just a brand; they tell a story about you. They build the "know, like and trust" factor with your audience.

This particular photo shoot was to take place out of town while I was speaking at an event, which forced me to narrow down my wardrobe selection in advance. I wanted to convey that I was real and authentic and also classy, fearless and feminine.

How does one communicate such a message in a simple photograph? It felt like the more appropriate attire would have been a business top and pretty pajama pants (like I wear as I work from home most days). But just to play it safe, I chose something neutral; black pants, a white top and a bright necklace for a splash of color.

And just as I was about to close my suitcase the playful side of me begged me to pack *the skirt*. I am sure you have one of them too… It's the one I had fallen in love with at the store and then hidden away at the back of my closet for over a year, waiting for the right moment to be worn. It was gorgeous! Royal blue, A-line style with bold flowers in pink, yellow and white. It screamed *"Here I am, look at me!"*

I packed the skirt before I could change my mind, all while secretly knowing it would likely remain unworn and unseen this time too.

Oddly enough, the day of the photo shoot I woke up with an extra pep in my step and decided to go for it. I put on the skirt I was brave enough to buy but hadn't quite been bold enough to wear, yet, and walked out the door.

I arrived for the photo shoot wearing that brilliant blue skirt, white classy top and hot pink heels, feeling like I could do anything. It was in that moment that I felt God whisper to my heart what I so badly needed to hear, *"Just be you, darling."*

The photos turned out beautiful, but the best part is that every time I look at them and see myself in the blue skirt that was begging to be worn, I see a girl who stood up tall, embraced her personality and allowed God to shine through her. It was a turning point in my business and my life.

In *Faith Like Flamingos* Katie is advocating for women, just like you and me, who need the gentle reminder to stand tall in who God has created us to be. Embracing your unique self may not look like putting on a royal blue skirt with festive flowery fabric and pink heels, but I would be willing to bet that much like my skirt, you have something hidden away inside that is just *begging* to be seen.

Katie's writing is both humorous and compelling as she calls us each to walk tall, embrace our God-given uniqueness, and fulfill our purpose in the bold color we've been gifted. It's my prayer that *every* woman gets a copy of this book in her hands and lets the lessons from God's Word change her business and her life.

Always cheering for you,
Rachael Joy Gilbert, Founder
RachaelGilbert.com

Intro: What's With the Flamingos?

"If you're always trying to be normal you'll never know how amazing you can be!"
- Maya Angelou

We live two hours away, but in all our eight years in the Yucatan Peninsula, we'd never been to see it for ourselves—until today.

I don't know what I expected really. I mean I'd seen flamingos in zoos before. I knew the approximate size, shape and color, but to to *see them in the wild*! This was going to be amazing!

There are only six species of flamingos in the world, and the few thousand who remain in North and Central America tend to migrate around, from South Florida, to the Caribbean, to Cuba, and back around, following seasons and food supplies.

From mid January to the end of February an estimated 35,000 fabulous pink birds call Celestún, a tiny village on the beach of the Yucatan Peninsula in Mexico, home. And we were finally going to see them!

We chartered a local fishing boat for the seven of us, my husband and I and our 5 kids, ages 5-13 at the time, and set out on our two hour tour... (Anyone else hearing refrains of Gilligan's Island with that? No? Just me? Ok, sorry. Back to the story - and spoiler alert - we didn't shipwreck. Though that would have been a fabulous adventure too, especially with crocs in the river as big as our boat... but I digress...)

Even before we rounded the turn from the shallow ocean bay into the mouth of the river, I spotted a few specs of pink on the ocean horizon.

"Funny" I thought. *"That they would be out in the open ocean."*

The guide pointed them out and said it was still shallow enough even that far out that they were standing in the water.

We entered the *Ria Celestún*, went under the only bridge from the mainland onto the sort -of island and then we saw them...

Pinky, coral colored puffs everywhere.

As far as the eye could see up river you saw water, pink cotton candy cloud looking dots and then the trees and sky. It was cool and yet *odd* at the same time. Strange and different from anything I'd ever seen before.

The guide slowed the boat as we approached a group of the fluffy pink things and their ridiculously long necks. "There are thousands here" he said. "Probably more than 20,000 have already arrived and in a couple of weeks we'll have over 35,000."

As he raised the outboard motor up out of the shallow water, to be sure we didn't hit a rock or something, he explained that here, where the fresh water from the river and the mangrove swamps (*manglares*) met the salt water of the sea, the water was shallow.

The flamingos use the shallows as feeding grounds, nesting grounds and security from predators (like crocodiles). They were not swimming. They were standing. Many of them with bodies at water level and some a bit taller.

There was no rush or flurry. The loud shiny boat didn't seem to scare them, and while they didn't run from us, neither did they approach us. The guide let our boat drift to within 10 feet of them. Again, I must admit, I don't know what I had been expecting, but this felt a bit anti-climactic.

They weren't scared, but neither were they curious or desiring to interact with us. They were just there, majestically beautiful and pink, oblivious to how much they stood out in the scenery and carrying on with their day as if we were invisible, gawking from our boat a few feet away.

Our tour took us then through a mangrove tunnel, to a fresh water pool (where we did see crocodiles!) and then back down the river to the ocean again.

As we picked up speed and headed back to the beach from which we'd embarked, salty wind swishing our hair around our faces, I thought about how so many of the women I serve are like flamingos—without even knowing it!

They are gorgeous! They are talented. They are loyal. They stand on their own two feet in spite of currents pushing against them. They care for others deeply. They're having an effect on the world around them - and yet, coming from how often I have to remind them of these things, they, like the flamingos, seem oblivious to how special, and fabulous they are!

This book is for you, my dear, dear flamingo-ish friend. To remind you, as a Christian in business, how fabulous you are. To encourage you to embrace your flamingo-like-ness. To walk tall, to appreciate and display your God-given uniqueness, and to use your bold colors to point others to the glory and fascinatingly perfect design of our all-good, Creator God.

All my love,
Katie

Section 1
It's OK to Be Pink

1.
Pink Blooded Birds

"Life's too short to be ordinary."

- Anonymous

I realize it's early in this relationship to be making assumptions, but I am going to assume that if you're reading this book you are already convinced that you have a message and a mission to share it with people. I am believing that you have a desire to multiply your influence and your impact, to reach more people all the time, and that you most likely have a movement waiting to happen.

But (and I realize its also early in the book to be saying but, but hear me out) ... if you will be successful with the message, mission and movement God is growing through you, you must first be willing to allow the inside out.

Here's what I mean: The flamingo's pink-ness isn't just a show he puts on. Flamingos are pink on the inside and out! Their feathers, skin, blood... it's all pink! And they're not ashamed to show it. You my beautiful friend should not be ashamed of who God made you to be either.

My husband and I were missionaries before we were business owners and during our first three years on the mission field, it was communicated to me repeatedly that loud colored clothes, nail polish, hair pieces, pins, jewelry etc were counterproductive to the Gospel. That their use was a selfish pitch for attention and a distraction from the work we were to be doing and the message we were to be giving. I took it to heart and stuffed the fun, bold colorful part of my personality (incidentally one of the things my husband first fell in love with) down into my floor length black skirts and complied. I had no desire to interfere with the work of the Gospel.

I would later learn that God doesn't make mistakes. In fact, your personality, your heart, your emotions, your quirks, your color.... all of that makes you *you*. It attracts others to you so you can share Christ with them, and makes you more capable of fulfilling God's plan for your life.

Listen to Genesis 1:21. And God created whales, and every living creature that moves, which the waters brought forth abundantly, after their kind, and every winged fowl after his kind: and God saw that it was good.

It was good. Did you catch that? It was good. The same word "good" that he uses to describe his creation of man a few verses later. God simply does not create junk, you included. You are "good" in God's eyes, with all of your idiosyncrasies and (what you think are) flaws.

And now hear this from 2 Samuel 22:20. He brought me forth also into a large place: he delivered me, because he delighted in me.

God has delivered you from eternal damnation, from yourself, from _____ (you fill in the blank) *because* he *delights* in you! He delights in *you*! He is a perfect God who makes no mistakes, he made you good, and he delights in you just the way he made you. How liberating is that! Long pink neck or not, you my friend, can walk tall today in the knowledge of this truth alone.

Years later, on a hot afternoon in a different ministry, in a desperate hurry I grabbed one of my daughter's headbands just before going live to teach a virtual class. Several students commented on the flower headband I'd grabbed without thought to fashion accessory, and the next week when I showed up without it, they wanted to know why...

Why not? I thought. I began to wear a flower headband more often, and then daily as God began to work in my heart and whisper that he delighted in me, and delighted in the way I felt when I wore something beautiful in my hair, I realized that the flower had become a symbol of his pleasure and an outward expression of the inward color I had for so long felt like I needed to suppress.

I can't tell you how many ministry and business conversations the Lord has opened to me since then *because* I am crowned with a flower symbol of the Lord's favor.

But maybe you still don't believe? Maybe you're thinking *"That's great for you Katie, you're beautiful, but does God know what I am like on the inside? Does he really want me to show that on the outside?"* The answer is yes! Better to show the ugly and deal with it, get forgiveness, let him wash it clean and paint you pretty again than to live as a hypocrite.

Here is what God had to say to the hypocrites of the Jesus' day: Woe unto you, scribes and Pharisees, hypocrites! for you are like unto whited sepulchers, (i.e. white painted tombs) which indeed appear beautiful outward, but are within full of dead men's bones, and of all uncleanness (Matthew 23:27).

That's strong language and makes it clear that God wants us to be genuine, not hiding who we really are or pretending to be something we're not. He made us 'good' remember! I shudder to think of all the opportunities to influence others for Christ that I missed during those years when I wasn't letting my true colors show.

Ephesians 2:10 says that we are his workmanship, created in Christ Jesus unto good works, which God has before ordained that we should walk in them.

He pre-ordained, pre-ordered, pre-meditated, planned intentionally and ahead of time the message and work he has for you and I to do! And it's a good work! Your message matters.

So let's review....
God doesn't make mistakes.
He made you "good."
He delights in you.
He wants you to be genuine, showing your inside colors on the outside.
He has a message for you to give and a plan for your life. A good work he wants you to do.

Wow! You are incredibly special! Take a moment to consider all that the God of the universe did for you and has planned for *you*!

To Consider:

If you're like me, after reading that, you may feel strongly that it is entirely appropriate to bow before our Creator God and thank him, right now.

Adore him. Worship him. Confess, if necessary,
And ask his help to live genuinely, like the flamingo: pink on the inside, pink on the outside. It doesn't matter if you meet a tourist or a crocodile, pink is what you're gonna get!

Note from Katie:
I am thrilled you've started this book! If the audio book would help you, I'd love to gift it to you FREE if you'll submit your purchase receipt to FLF@katiehornor.com

I highly recommend spending some time journaling and praying through the "To Consider" sections at the end of each chapter. Make some notes about what God is speaking to you through his Word, and the steps he wants you to take next.

If you'd like to deepen your study, you can purchase the companion Bible study guide or a flamingo journal for note taking at KatieHornor.com/FLFResources.

2.
You Are What You Eat

"You cannot hide whats inside, it's sure to come out."

-Ron Hamilton, Patch the Pirate

The flamingos' fabulous pink color is due in part to their regular diet of crustaceans. The betacarotene they ingest in those foods colors their blood, their flesh and their feathers.

There is a fabulous children's book by Jennifer Sattler that gives a vivid portrait of just what this looks like. In the book, *Sylvie* the flamingo has a desire for a more glamorous diet.[1] She tries eating

---

[1] Find the book *Sylvie* at KatieHornor.com/FLFResources

stripes and turns striped. She tries eating dots and ends up speckled. She tries eating blue like the sky and ends up blue… This experiment continues until *Sylvie* has a stomach ache and arrives at the conclusion that the diet God intended for her is best. The diet you feed yourself shows, my friend, and it shows in your business too.

You may not be a flamingo eating shrimp, but a constant diet of comparison leaves you grumpy and whiny which in reality is discontent with God's plan for you. You begin thinking you know better than he and questioning his sovereignty and goodness.

A diet of lies, complaints, and jealousy leaves you physically sick in many instances.

A diet of fear forgets who is in charge, whose business this is anyway, who sees what is coming and who is in complete control at *every step*.

By feasting on the Word of God, getting to know him, maturing in him, 1 Peter 2:1-3 says that we will grow and we will taste of his graciousness and that he will shine through us to all we meet in life and in business.

Once someone of obvious New Age beliefs approached me at a business conference saying,

"I've been watching you I just had to meet you! You radiate peacefulness and light! What is your secret to such calm?"

I then was able to share with her that it's Christ in me and his peace that she was seeing.

Proverbs 15:13 tells us that a merry heart makes a cheerful countenance. If your heart is not happy in your Lord, it shows on your face, both at home and at work.

One of my favorite quotes of all times is from Ken Collier the Director of The Wilds Christian Camp and Conference Center:[2]

> **YOU DO WHAT YOU DO AND YOU SAY WHAT YOU SAY BECAUSE YOU THINK WHAT YOU THINK.**
>
> **YOU THINK WHAT YOU THINK BECAUSE YOU BELIEVE WHAT YOU BELIEVE ABOUT GOD, HIS WORD AND YOURSELF.**

You do what you do and you say what you say because you think what you think. And you think what you think because you believe what you believe about God, his Word and yourself.

---

[2] The Wilds Christian Camp and Conference Center https://wilds.org

This is why I like to start each year off taking students through our *Doing Business, with God* course.[3] I spend 6 weeks with a a group of Christian business owners just like you, taking a deep dive together into God's truth about himself, his Word, and his plan for your life and your business. It refocuses me, and my students and grounds our beliefs and thoughts in truth as we make plans for the new year.

Whether we like it or not what's on the inside of us does come out. Just as it showed on *Sylvie* the flamingo, it shows in your actions, in your words, and in your countenance, flowing through to your business as well.

To Consider:
What have you been feeding on lately? Are you showing your true healthy pink from feeding on God's truth or are you a bit striped and in need of getting back to the diet that was meant for you?

---

[3] Doing Business, with God https://bloggingsuccessfully.com/courses

3.
Ugly Feature or Super Power?

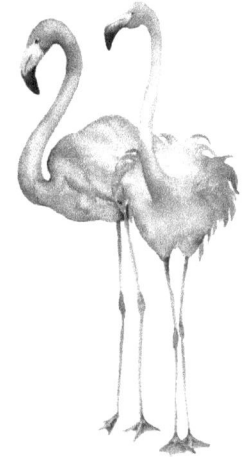

"What bothers you as your greatest quirk, could turn out to be a super power if you alter how you think about it and what you do with it."

- Katie Hornor

The flamingo has webbed feet different from many other winged species. They also have long gangly thin legs. They can't take off immediately from standing and fly. And yet they don't hang their head bemoaning their differences from other birds—do you know why?

Those webbed feet and gangly bending backward legs allow them to walk in water deeper than other birds can, stirring up the silt at the bottom in search of food. They allow them to run on the surface of the water and take flight to escape their predators, or to move on to the next food location.

If birds could talk I'd imagine flamingos might take a bit of harassing from other birds in the wild because of their "weirdness." But flamingos embrace God's quirky design for them because it is his way of providing for and protecting them!

Once, a ministry leader said to us: "*I know you serve the same God, but you just do it very differently than we do.*"

At the time, I thought it was a derogatory remark, but I've since learned to appreciate that when you're led by the Spirit in your life *and* in your business, you do things that at times appear quirky and weird to others.

Our "serving differently" at that time, and the subsequent rejection from that particular leader, and others who followed their leadership, protected my husband and I from a lifetime of missing God's perfect plan for us.

What is it that you feel like is quirky, gangly or weird about how God made you or the abilities he's given you? Have you ever stopped to think that it was on purpose? By design? To give you a special edge in life and even to provide for you or to protect you?

Ecclesiastes 3:11 says, He {God} has made everything beautiful in his time.

And that *everything* includes you my quirky friend.

According to Romans 12:6, we each have different gifts according to his divine enablement (grace) in our lives. God doesn't want us to all be the same. He wants us to embrace our uniqueness.

2 Peter 3:18 tells us that we are to grow in grace, and in the knowledge of our Lord and Savior Jesus Christ. When you know God, his *grace* (divine enablement and unmerited favor) and his *peace* are multiplied unto you. His grace mixed with the quirks he designed, and the peace that comes from knowing him can only serve to bring him glory.

To Consider:
Have you been complaining over a certain quality, physical characteristic, ability or disability that God's given you? Have you been questioning why you are so different from others in your neighborhood, niche, industry, office or organization? Isn't it time you embraced your unique feature as your super power? As a gift from your Creator God?

I thank God for making you different, beautifully quirky, and I encourage you to look for ways you can uniquely excel and bring him glory in that!

4.
Pink and Not Sorry

"In a world where you can be anything... be yourself."

- Anonymous

The pink flamingo is not sorry he's pink. He doesn't walk around apologizing to his own kind or to other animals because his crazy colors upset the natural blues and greens of the landscape. He doesn't even worry about his color making him a target for predators... What if it does make him a target? God's created a way of escape (he can run on water and fly away because of his quirky webbed feet, remember?)

Flamingos live in the open, in plain sight, in large numbers, showing off their God-given colors and doing life as they were designed to without apology, and unashamed.

Psalm 25:20 says, O keep my soul, and deliver me: let me not be ashamed; for I put my trust in you.

As a Christian in the business world, we bring glory to our Lord when we show who we are on the inside on the outside, without fear.

> **AS A CHRISTIAN IN THE BUSINESS WORLD, WE BRING GLORY TO OUR LORD WHEN WE SHOW WHO WE ARE ON THE INSIDE ON THE OUTSIDE WITHOUT FEAR.**

Someone once told me I should keep my "God talk" out of my business. That I should separate my faith from my work. That's a bit like trying to separate the yellow from an egg yolk.

There is no need to walk around apologizing for your faith—though neither should you cram the pink crustacean food of the Word down the throats of others who are not ready for it.

Timothy tells us not to be ashamed of the testimony of our Lord (2 Timothy 1:8). Like Paul in Romans 1:16 we can say, I am not ashamed of the Gospel of Christ: for it is the power of God unto salvation to every one that believes.

Following Jesus openly and living for him in the workplace will sometimes create "situations," just as I'm sure being a pink bird in the open expanse of a crocodile infested river does. After all, in Matthew 10:16, Christ said that he is sending us forth as sheep in the midst of wolves. And that therefore, we should live "wise as serpents, but harmless as doves."

Our Christianity may very well make us a target, but we must not fear God's design or his plan, because he is in control and has overcome the world. Walking with him and unashamedly doing what he's created us for and called us to is the best place in the world we could possibly be.

To Consider:

Are you now, or have you been, ashamed to show the true colors of your faith in the workplace? Could the frustration you've been feeling be stemming from the fact that you're trying to hide who you are on the inside?

Take a few moments to bare your heart to the Lord, ask for his help, his courage and his peace to fulfill your purpose in bold color.

5.
Perfectly Awkward

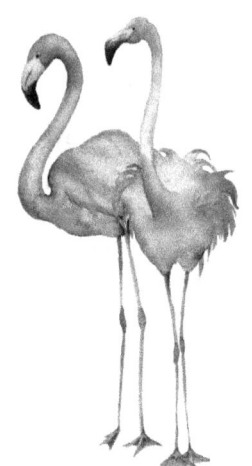

"You are not perfect. And that is perfectly fine."
- Anonymous

Four to five feet tall, but only four to eight pounds, the flamingo and all his pink plumage is specially designed for life in the water and in the air.

If he looks funny wading in the river, sleeping on one leg, sitting on a muddy pile of a nest, he looks even more comical flying through the air with long neck sticking out in front and long legs dangling behind.

And yet, God's design is *perfect* for his life. And so is his design for yours, my friend.

When I was a child and was feeling wistful or hopeful about the future, I often found myself drawing the same picture: It was a sailboat on a calm sea with the sun dipping below the horizon under a beautiful clear sky.

Nothing particularly funny about that unless you consider that I grew up in the mountains of western North Carolina. We had to cross at least 2 mountains to go anywhere. I'd been to the beach for a whole 3 hours as a child, and I'd never seen the sunset over the water (lake or ocean) until I was in college.

I am sure it looked funny to some that a mountain raised, free-range child would consistently draw a picture of a sunset by the sea. Even to me it felt odd that this mental image would be the one that represented peace to my soul. It was awkward anytime someone asked about it. But it was what my soul kept going back to every time I needed a visual of peace.

Take a moment to digest these truths:
God knew you and had a plan for you before you were conceived in your mother's womb (Jeremiah 1:5).

God saw in the beginning everything he had made, including man and woman, and "behold, it was very good" (Genesis 1:31).

Deuteronomy 32:4 tells us that God is the Rock, his work is perfect; for all his ways are judgement: A God of truth and without iniquity, just and right is he.

The Psalmist says, I will praise you; for I am fearfully and wonderfully made (Psalm 139:14).

And Ecclesiastes 7:8 says, Better is the end of a thing than the beginning thereof: and the patient in spirit is better than the proud in spirit.

The end of the story?

When I was 39, my husband and I were walking hand in hand along the boardwalk in our coastal town in the south of Mexico taking in the sunset. The sea was calm. The smell of salt was slight in the friendly breeze that played at the hem of my skirt; and the sky that night was brushed with colors only God has in his paint box. We sat down on the sea wall to bask in the sizzle of the sun against the glassy horizon as it begin to dip into the sea — when I realized...

This was the exact picture I had drawn so often, so many years ago.

The master artist had placed within the heart of a small girl from the mountains a foreshadowing of his work; a longing for what he would call me to do and a where he would take me to live. I was living out in real life the peaceful image he had spoken to my heart through that favorite drawing so long ago.

Awe washed over me as I realized - *I was made to live here. To do this!*

What a wonderful and beautiful assurance of his love for me; a confirmation of his will in guiding me through the journey of mountains and deserts, hurts and healings that had led me here.[4]

Just as for the flamingo, God's design for you, my friend, was created before your conception. His plan for you is just as amazing, if not more so, than that of the perfectly awkward yet dazzling flamingo.

That desire or talent or knowledge or insight that you have that feels awkward now — I am confident that God sees it as part of the perfect work he is working in you.

It's my opinion that sometimes our God-designed awkwardness is simply a way to keep us humble until he reveals his plan. It shows us that we need him, and his peace, every moment of every day.

---

[4] Follow my instagram https://instagram.com/katiehornor to see my sunset photos in #Campechebythesea

> **GOD'S DESIGN FOR YOU, MY FRIEND, WAS CREATED BEFORE YOUR CONCEPTION.**

To Consider:

Is there anything in your life that you can look back on and see how God used it to prepare you for something that came later?

What is your perfectly awkward characteristic? or ability? Can you give it to the Lord? Can you admit you don't understand why, but that you are willing to accept his grace for imperfection, stop guilting yourself over what you see as a flaw, and wait until the day he might reveal the reason?

Can you praise him for how he made you? Awkwardness, imperfections and all?

Section 2
Live in Bold Color

6.
You're Not Extinct!

"If you're still breathing, there is still a job for you to do and a purpose for your life."
- Katie Hornor

There are six species of flamingos in the world. None of them are extinct. It would be silly for one group to simply stop eating, stop defending their nests, stop migrating to the next place because "other flamingos are doing it too."

If that example sounds ludicrous, it's because it is!

It's just as silly for you to think that your talent or genius or gift is not needed because you know of one or two other "birds" doing the same thing.

Often I hear my Blog Connection or mastermind members say something like *"but I can't do _____ because so-and-so is already doing it."*

We (myself included) are so easily intimidated thinking about the "others" and their work that it distracts us from *our* calling!

My client, Brenda[5] started out intimidated to share her message about the freedom of breaking the Clutter Code Chains and decluttering your home and life to better fulfill your purpose. But now that she's touching thousands with her best-selling book and course, and speaking on stages across the country, she's shared with me that she's thankful she stepped up to help those who need her expertise.

The truth is *you* are not extinct!

You're still here, and if God has called you to do _____, it doesn't matter how many others are doing that or doing something similar, there is still a need for *you* to do it too.

---

[5] Brenda Mason, Tiny House Sweetheart, Downsizing31.com

God can use *each* of us, and he has a plan for each person's specific talents. There is still work for *you* to do or you simply would not still be here.

2 Corinthians 10:12 tells us that when we measure or compare ourselves among ourselves "we are unwise."

You are *you*, not them. You have unique
- Personality
- Life Experiences
- Training
- Viewpoint
- Talent
- Sense of Humor
- Communication Skills...

Your very uniqueness *demands* that you also teach or do what you've been given to do because not everyone will be able to learn from "the other bird."

They are unique too. Some people will resonate with them, but all of them won't. Some are waiting for *you* to teach them. They won't ever learn, grow, or get the transformation without you. Have you ever stopped to think that you may be hurting them by just thinking about yourself?

That's right. When you're thinking about the competition, and all the reasons why you shouldn't go ahead and do what God's asking you to do, you're being selfish, thinking about yourself, instead of about all of the people who need what you have to offer!

If you change the way you think, and who you're thinking about you will soon realize that there are many ways to teach and to learn. You might even end up thankful for those other teachers because you'll realize that with you reaching your people and them reaching their people you collectively are now impacting *more* people than if one of you didn't act because you feared "competing."

John 9:4 says, I must work the works of him who sent me because the night cometh when no man can work.

> **IF YOU'RE STILL BREATHING, THERE IS STILL A JOB FOR YOU TO DO AND A PURPOSE FOR YOUR LIFE.**

Focus on those who need you rather than on those who also serve those people, and remember that this is all about living as God has designed *you* to live—for his glory.

1 Corinthians 10:31 says, Whether therefore you eat or drink, or *whatsoever* you do, do all to the glory of God.

To Consider:

What or who has been holding you back from doing what you know God wants you to do? Have you been focused on the "competition" more than on the people who need the transformation you offer/teach?

Fear of man can be debilitating and sabotaging...

Ask God now to forgive your fear of man and give you a renewed focus on the people who need you and your work.

7.
Lead Pinky!

"A good leader is one who, knows the way, goes the way and shows the way."

- John C. Maxwell

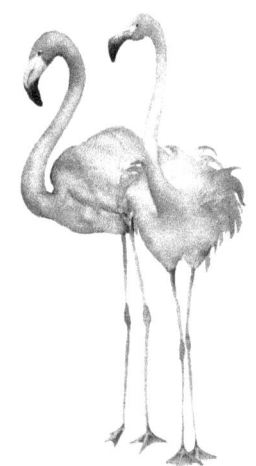

Among a flock of flamingos, you can spot the leader by his color. He's the pinkest. He has proven that he can find the best foods, not just in words, but in physical evidence. The more he eats the good pink crustaceans the more pink he becomes both on the inside and outside. His pinkness sets him apart and others look to him as the leader.[6]

---

[6] https://www.discoverwildlife.com/animal-facts/birds/facts-about-flamingo/

If we translate this into the daily life and activities of a Christian in business, the one who is most like Christ, most fed by the Spirit will be the better servant leader.

Just like the flamingo leader, the human leader will lead others to the "good food" of the Word of God. He will always be pointing them back to the Truth of Christ and always encouraging them to a healthier relationship with God.

John 3:30 says, He {God} must increase, I must decrease.

When we were newly married, my husband's construction job boss was a believer and took a special interest in mentoring him. It was obvious he knew God, and honored him with his time, his talk and his revenues. We wanted to be savvy like him. It was his generosity and leadership that introduced us to Dave Ramsey's work[7] and ministry of Financial Peace University. His faith and example influenced our being able to pay off our college debts and move overseas debt free.

As a Christian in business you want to be feeding on the Word so much that it's obvious on the outside. So much that others look at you and see Christ, just like we look at the flamingo leader and see pink.

---

[7] Dave Ramsey, DaveRamsey.com

When you have the mind of Christ you will have these leadership qualities which are all evidenced by actions (Philippians 2:1-5):

1. Leaders will comfort
2. Leaders will love
3. Leaders will have fellowship with the Spirit
4. Leaders will show mercy
5. Leaders will seek agreement (peace) over disagreement (#BetterTogether)
6. Leaders will not strive (argue/fight) with others (#CollaborateDontCompete)
7. Leaders will not seek their own glory/reputation
8. Leaders will seek other's benefits before their own (#PeopleOverProfit)
9. Leaders will care about others
10. Leaders will not be selfish

Interestingly enough, the traits the modern world identifies as leadership skills are eerily missing from the list I just shared. No where in that list do we see being strong, unbending, competitive, focused on growth, firm...

> **GOD'S WAY OF LEADERSHIP IS *SERVANT* LEADERSHIP. FIND THE WAY, AND SHEPHERD OTHERS TO FIND THE WAY WITH YOU.**

That's not to say there's something wrong with being strong, desiring growth etc, but God's way of leadership is *servant* leadership and is action based and others oriented. Find the way, and shepherd others to find the way with you.

To Consider:

Are you feeding yourself on the "best food"? How will you lead others to Christ if you are not walking close to him yourself?

How many of the above characteristics do you regularly show in your business relationships and interactions? Which one could you work on improving this week?

Ask God to help you be a servant leader and make this a regular part of your life as you grow to be more like him.

8.
Do the Mating Dance

"You absolutely can do everything you want to do, just not all at the same time."

- Katie Hornor

Flamingos don't mate all year round. They will mate once per year during the rainy season. During mating you'll find them doing a silly little dance to disrupt the calm and attract the attention of would-be partners.

In business we also have silly little dances we do to attract the attention of would-be clients and promotional partners. We call our dances by such names as promotions, webinars, advertising, campaigns, opt-ins, funnels, etc.

Once upon a time, for a period of about five years, The Blog Connection, my membership site for new to intermediate bloggers[8], was open all year round. All year I was trying to both serve my members and trying to promote to new members. It was exhausting and I wasn't doing a very good job of attracting new members or serving my current ones.

One day I read Ecclesiastes 3:1 which says, to every thing there is a season, and a time to every purpose under the heaven.

When I started thinking about what I was doing in my business in light of what I'd learned of the flamingo life cycle and this Scripture, I had a lightbulb moment.

Of course it's exhausting to attract attention and grow the relationship into a commitment all the time! Even birds are smarter than that!

> **IT'S POSSIBLE YOU COULD SERVE YOUR PEOPLE BETTER BY CREATING SEASONAL ACTIVITIES OR RHYTHMS IN YOUR BUSINESS.**

---

[8] TheBlogConnection.com

It's possible you could serve your people better by creating seasonal activities or rhythms in your business.

Promotions could be for a season, so that once the relationship is secured, you spend your time in the next season nurturing the relationship.

I moved to promoting The Blog Connection[9] a few times per year, closing the ability to join in the meantime so that I can focus my efforts on nurturing those members and growing them into who they need to be as online business owners. It totally changes the energy going into both activities when they each have their own assigned season.

To Consider:

Are you trying to make everything happen in your business all at once? Could you (and your business) benefit from creating seasonal activities or rhythms?

Ask the Lord for wisdom as you take a look at your promotions and your post-promotion responsibilities to your customers and clients... Could you serve them better by creating seasons in your business?

---

[9] TheBlogConnection.com

9.
A Single Focus

"To be truly effective, your daily activity must align with your long-term vision, strategies. and tactics."

- Brian P. Moran

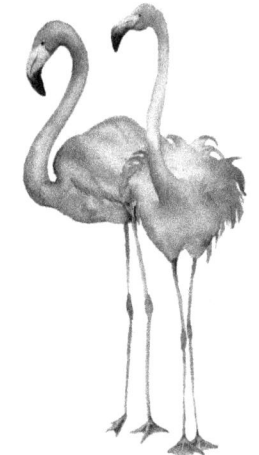

Flamingo couples only lay one single egg per year. Both parents share the responsibility of sitting on it. Both share the responsibility of feeding the hatched baby. Once the egg is laid they have a single united focus: get this baby to adulthood.

What is your single focus in your business? Do you know what it is? Do your helpers, assistants, contractors, board members (i.e. family members) know what that one main focus is? Are you motivating the whole team to work in alignment with that single focus goal? Ephesians 4:16 tells us that the whole body is filthy joined together and compacted by that which every joint supplies, according to the effectual working in the measure of every part, making increase of the body unto the edifying of itself.

Some call this a vision statement, a 10-year goal, a 3-year goal, a quarterly goal, a "big rock"...

Each quarter my husband and I have a special date. We go somewhere away from our house, kids and office for a quarterly planning date. We talk through long term and short term dreams, bucket list items, goals and action steps for the family and the business. We review our calendars together, delegate tasks and address any issues that have come up.

As I am the more visible personality in our business (teaching, writing, speaking) and he is the behind the scenes power (tech support, customer service, order fulfillment) our quarterly planning session helps us tremendously to stay on the same page, work consistently towards our common goals and present a unified front to our children and to the clients and contractors who may answer to each of us separately.

When each member of your business knows their part and what the common goal is that you're all working towards it's much easier to effectively work together toward that goal.

It's also easier to keep distractions in check, and chart your progress toward success when you have a single focus and well defined goal.

It's up to you, as the leader to clearly communicate the common goal and ensure that each one's responsibilities are assigned and explained. It's also important to encourage them in their own special role in the teamwork.

To Consider:
Do you have a clearly defined focus or goal in your business? Do those who work with you know what it is and understand how their work fits into that single focus and helps the business as a whole reach that goal?

What could you do differently to ensure that you're all working together with your individual jobs and talents towards that goal?

10.
Pinker than You

"A teacher is successful when his student surpasses him and goes on to be a successful teacher of the next generation."
- Katie Hornor

Flamingo parents feed their young until they are mature and it takes nearly all the color from their feathers.

Flamingos are among a select few birds that feed their young directly from a secretion produced in their crop (throat), and this 'crop milk' is bright pink. It's interesting that so much carotenoid is used up by their crop milk that by the end of a breeding season parents of both sexes have lost the pink coloring from their feathers and appear almost white.[10]

To translate this into business terms, to have a successful generational impact, you need to give all you've got to your people. The goal is to make them "pinker" than you, to make them successfully mature in your area of expertise, to make them the teachers of next generation. You *want* your students, customers and clients to pass you up, for this is proof of your success.

In 2 Timothy 2:2 Paul tells his student Timothy: the things that you have heard of me among many witnesses, the same commit {teach} to faithful men {people}, who will be able to teach others also.

We teach what we've been given to perpetuate the teaching of that skill or truth to the next generation. Our success is in giving our all so that the next generation can be successful in teaching the next generation and so on… Why?

Titus 2:3-5 fills this in… the older women are instructed to
- Be in behavior as becomes holiness,
- Not false accusers,
- Not given to much wine,
- Teachers of good things;

---

[10] https://www.discoverwildlife.com/animal-facts/birds/facts-about-flamingo/

{so} that {you} may teach the young women
- To be sober,
- To love their husbands,
- To love their children,
- To be discreet,
- Chaste,
- Keepers at home,
- Good,
- Obedient to their own husbands,

that the Word of God be not blasphemed.

Did you catch that? We are to teach others what we've learned to do so "that the Word of God be not blasphemed." So that no one can look at us and find fault with God's Word or his plan.

> **A TEACHER IS SUCCESSFUL WHEN HIS STUDENT SURPASSES HIM AND GOES ON TO TEACH THE NEXT GENERATION.**

Our giving our all to teach the next generation what we've been given to teach, our helping them be successful, has a direct impact on God's reputation among those who do not know him.

The adult flamingo gives his all to make his offspring a successful, mature, adult bird. The young bird's color is a public testament to the care and nurturing of the parents.

Similarly, your excellence in your work, your dedication to the success of your students, customers and clients, your care for those you serve is evident. Their ability is your success. Are you making them pinker than you?

To Consider:
How do you define success? Have you ever defined it in terms of the success of your students? In terms of your impact on future generations?

Have you ever considered that as a Christian your work has a direct impact on God's reputation among those who do not yet know him as Savior?

Take some time today to prayerfully consider your definition of success and the legacy impact you want to leave on the next generation.

Note from Katie:
I hope you're enjoying this book. I'd love to hear your definition of success. I believe it's different for each of us, and important that we define it so we can

know when we reach it. If you want to share yours with me, post it on social and use the hashtag #FaithLikeFlamingos.

Get the *Bible Study* guide for individuals & groups, or the *Faith Like Flamingos Journal* at FaithLikeFlamingos.com.

Forward the purchase receipt of this book to FLF@katiehornor.com to get the audio book FREE!

CLAIM YOUR FREE AUDIO BOOK!

Section 3
Join the Flamboyance

11.
The Flamboyance Life

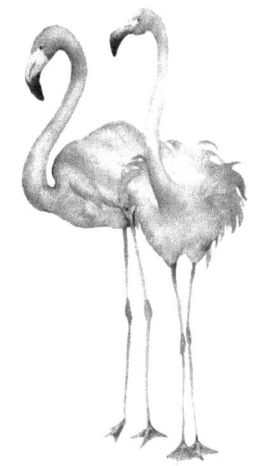

"Cheering someone else's success will never diminish yours. We are #BetterTogether."
- Katie Hornor

Both *flamingo* and *flamboyance* come from words referring to fire. Flamingo comes from the Spanish *flamenco* and Portuguese *flamengo*, literally, "flame-colored." *Flamboyance* comes from French, meaning "to flame" or "flair".[11] In our modern day language, being flamboyant means being colorful and vibrant but a group of flamingos is called a *flamboyance*.

---

[11] https://www.dictionary.com/e/s/flamboyance-flamingos-brilliant-bird-groups/#a-flamboyance-of-flamingos

A flamboyance of flamingos can be made up of anywhere from a couple dozen birds, to thousands of flamingos. If you've ever seen them in the wild, a flaming pink cloud against a canvas of blue and green, then you understand this term completely. One pink bird them would be unique, but a whole host of them together really make an impressive scene.

Flamingos don't have very many natural predators, in spite of their color which makes them an obvious target. In Africa they may face wild dogs, large cats, or pythons from which the best protection is a quick flight. Larger birds, such as storks or vultures, who would prey on the flamingo eggs or young can be thwarted when the birds band together in large groups protecting the nesting grounds.

It reminds me of Proverbs 11:14 which says, where no counsel is the people fall: but in the multitude of counsellors there is safety.

And Proverbs 24:6, for by wise counsel you will make war: and in the multitude of counsellors there is safety.

We spent the first four years of our business going it alone. We could not seem to find a community that understood the struggles of bootstrapping and growing an online business with the heart and vision we had. We had no one we could trust with our questions, stresses or drafted plans for growth. What's more, the communities of bloggers we did find were often filled with complaining, excuse-making, jealous, click-ey individuals who were more than willing to ask for favors, but rarely willing to give help.

In a "well if I can't find one, I'll create my own" moment I opened The Blog Connection to our first 20 members in 2015.

From those first 20, we built a community that has become a thriving, protective, nourishing flamboyance of bloggers (and when I say bloggers I mean online business owners, because if you have a site with a blog, or a blog with products, or a store with a site - it's all business).

These ladies rally around each other, encourage each other's big ideas, cheer each other's successes, sound the alarm when danger is lurking and come to the defense of their own when necessary. They grow together, problem solve together, cry together and celebrate together. They review each other's work, promote each other's products and courses. They are #BetterTogether ....

> **THERE IS PROTECTION, WISDOM, AND SAFETY TO BE FOUND IN A GROUP OF LIKEMINDED INDIVIDUALS WITH DIFFERENT LIFE EXPERIENCES, TALENTS AND EXPERTISE TO DRAW FROM.**

There is protection, wisdom, and safety to be found in a group of likeminded individuals with different life experiences, talents and expertise to draw from. It's what I envisioned a community to be and I am so in love with them and grateful for each one. It thrills me to see the color and wisdom they add to the group.

To Consider:

Do you play well with others? Do you work well as a team for the protection of all? Do you encourage the others who serve the same people you do. After all, you can't possibly reach *everyone* in the world who needs your message. God has put many of you to the task of reaching those who are prepared to hear from each of you. And think of how much more you could do if you worked together instead of against each other.

How could you put aside your pride and collaborate with someone in your niche instead of competing? How could you find a way to complement their offer with your own to serve your (collective) audience better?

It is good for you to look out for others as well as care for your own endeavors. If you don't currently have a flamboyance, check out the list of recommended mastermind groups at KatieHornor.com/FLFresources.

12.
A Pink Ballet

"Never doubt that a small group of thoughtful, committed citizens can change the world; indeed, it's the only thing that ever has."

– Margaret Mead

Flamingos are gregarious birds that do not do well in very small flocks of just a few birds. While a typical flock is only several dozen birds, flocks of up to a million or more have been recorded. Flamingos use these tremendous flamboyances as a safety measure against predators, and larger groups are more stable for population growth and breeding success.[12]

---

[12] https://www.thespruce.com/fun-facts-about-flamingos-385519

When you see flamingos on the move you often see them moving together as one giant body of birds. If one moves into the water, several will join him. If one takes flight, the entire flamboyance may take flight. Though they may be fleeing danger together, it appears to be a beautifully choreographed pink ballet.

1 Thessalonians 5:21-23 tells us to prove all things; hold fast that which is good. Abstain from all appearance of evil. And the very God of peace sanctify you wholly; and I pray God your whole spirit and soul and body be preserved blameless unto the coming of our Lord Jesus Christ.

Just as the flamingo who resists the urge to flee danger with the rest of the group, may not live to tell about it, so the Christian in business who does not flee the temptation to compromise his standards or beliefs may fall prey to the enemy's wiles.

Scripture tells us to "prove" or test things. Hang on to what is good, and abstain from evil and even the *appearance* of evil. Why? So we can be preserved blameless in spirit, soul and body.

And the next verse is perhaps my favorite of all time. Verse 24: Faithful is he that calls you, who also will do it.

Where do we get the strength to resist temptations and flee evil? From the One who called us to do it.

> **I BELIEVE GOD IS CALLING US, AS CHRISTIANS IN BUSINESS, TO BAND TOGETHER, TO TAKE FLIGHT TOGETHER AWAY FROM THE DANGERS OF PRIDE, FAKE-NESS, COMPARISON, COMPETITION, STANDARD PRACTICE AND MISLEADING MARKETING, AMONG OTHER THINGS.**

Business owners who have good morals, good ethics, high standards, keep their word etc., are nearly extinct in todays society. Aaron Walker[13], a popular Christian business coach, says: *"Isolation is the enemy of excellence."*

I believe God is calling us, as Christians in business, to band together, to take flight together away from the dangers of pride, fake-ness, comparison, competition, standard practice and misleading marketing (among other things).

If we want our business reputation and our testimony in the marketplace to reflect Christ, to succeed, and endure, we must rise above the appearance of evil, and of mediocrity. We must resist justifying doing things "just okay" because that's "the way everyone's doing it now." We must embrace the goodness and excellence that comes from our Father's example and his standards for life and business and influence other Christians to rise with us.

---

[13] Aaron Walker, ViewFromTheTop.com

The good news is that God promises to help us do it (1 Thessalonians 5:24).

To Consider:

Have you been tempted to cut corners, give okay service, create misleading marketing, or disregard rules or guidelines that govern your industry?

Have you been standing dangerously close to jealousy, inauthenticity, or mediocrity?

Do you need to ask forgiveness of the Lord or someone else for something you've done or for a misleading appearance you've created?

What steps can you take to flee those dangers from now on?

How can you create a culture of excellence in the way you do business and serve your clients, customers, partners and shareholders (family members) into the future?

What could you do to encourage your contemporaries, partners, and those in your social network to move as one in the direction of safety and excellence in business?

13.
Your Goose Honk

"Not everyone gets what you do. It's ok. Those who need your message will, and they will be grateful you didn't quit."
– Katie Hornor

Flamingos sound like geese when honking in a group. If you've never heard them, and are curious, look it up online and listen. It's a comical sound.

At a few days old, the white fluffy flamingo chick leaves the nest to join a small group of chicks. Parents work with the other parents to take turns watching the young and going out to look for food.

Upon their return, flamingo parents identify their chick by its voice.[14]

When I heard that fact, the Lord immediately brought to mind John 10:27 where Jesus says,

"My sheep hear my voice, and I know them, and they follow me: and I give unto them eternal life, and no man can take them out of my hand. My Father, which gave them me, is greater than all; and no man is able to pluck them out of my Father's hand. I and my Father are one."

> **YOUR PEOPLE WILL FOLLOW YOU FOR *YOUR* VOICE, *YOUR* MESSAGE, *YOUR* WAY OF DELIVERING WHAT THEY NEED.**

In a cacophony of other goose honks your voice will stand out to them, resonate with them, call to them and they will be nourished by what you bring them. Your people will follow you for *your* voice, *your* message, *your* way of delivering what they need.

There may be others nearby who are older, younger, taller, fatter, thinner, pinker, whiter, smarter, cuter, more experienced, more educated, better prepared (I think you get the idea) .... than you.

---

[14] https://kids.nationalgeographic.com/animals/birds/flamingo/

But God hasn't given your people to them. He gave them to *you*, and prepared *you* to serve them specifically.

Multiple people who have come into our community and courses through the years who shared with me that they tried to learn blogging or business from this or that other expert in the field, and just couldn't. The other teacher didn't explain clearly enough, or they didn't provide enough support, or they … the list goes on and on.

Does that mean the others are bad at teaching? No, it just means that different people will learn from different people. Your learning style, teaching style, life experiences, communication methods etc. will allow you to impact those God has specifically prepared for you to serve.

Think of what might happen if those flamingo parents fail to return to the creche and nourish their chick. Who else will do it? Who else knows his voice? Answers his call? None of the other birds do. They're caring for their own chick.

You must get your message out there. Someone, who can only be nourished by what you bring, is waiting for you. Looking for you. Praying right now that you will show up and do what you were created to do.

"I don't know how" you say? Ask the Lord. Here are his promises to you:

If any of you lack wisdom, let him ask of God, that gives to all men liberally, and upbraids {reprimands} not; and it shall be given him (James 1:5).

Call unto me, and I will answer you, and show you great and mighty things, which you knew not (Jeremiah 33:3).

I love the Lord, because he has heard my voice and my supplications (Psalm 116:1).

Don't make excuses. You can do this. You were created for this!

Don't get distracted. Don't play with danger. Don't dillydally or delay. The success of the next generation is depending on you reaching them with your message. #YourMessageMatters.

To Consider:
What is your message?
Who is your message for?
Why will they resonate with you instead of some "other bird?"
What makes your goose honk different?
What will their life be like if you don't help them?

How will their life be different once they have implemented your help?

What is holding you back from sharing your message?

What is the first step, something you can do today, to get your message out to one who needs it?

14.
Delight in the Mud

"No mud can soil us but the mud we throw."

– James Russell Lowell

Flamingos tend to congregate in mudflats, lagoons, or river deltas where they can find shallow saltwater prey. They are good swimmers and flyers, but prefer to stand in shallow water, where predators are clearly seen and warned as these muddy habitats are difficult for predators to navigate.[15]

---

[15] https://www.mentalfloss.com/article/61853/15-fascinating-flamingo-facts

Most Christian business owners I know will tell you they don't like the mud, i.e the messy parts of their lives or business. But what if that's where you are meant to thrive? What if that is part of God's sovereign design for you and/or his protection over you?

Proverbs 3:26 says, For the Lord shall be your confidence, and shall keep your foot from being taken.

And in Psalm 40:1-3 we read: I waited patiently for the Lord; and he inclined unto me, and heard my cry. He brought me up also out of an horrible pit, out of the miry clay (mud), and set my feet upon a rock, and established my goings. And he has put a new song in my mouth, even praise unto our God: many will see it, and fear, and will trust in the Lord.

When we see the flamingo, his unique design and habitat, we praise the Lord for making such a beautiful thing—even though we know he lives in mud! We recognize that the muddy habitat is part of God's plan for the flamingo, part of God's protection on his life. Out there in the open, in the mud, the flamingo thrives, and displays his colors openly for all the world to see.

> **YOU ARE NEVER SAFER THAN WHEN YOU ARE DOING EXACTLY WHAT THE LORD HAS CALLED YOU TO DO.**

When folks want to bring up "mud" in our lives, they point to letters sent by a mission board slandering us to our supporters. They point to dreams dashed when a lifetime of orphan ministry was pulled out from under us. They point to betrayal by national pastors and 6 years of church planting efforts with only a handful of decisions for Christ and a congregation made up of our family and the occasional visitor. They point to the loss of emotional and financial support from family and friends who once believed in us. These are parts of our story that are messy, but so totally God-ordained that we would not be standing where we are today, serving God in the way he created us to serve him in a ministry and business that now reaches around the world had we not first been led through the mud.[16]

> **LIVING IN YOUR ZONE OF GENIUS MAY BE MUDDY, BUT IT IS WHERE YOU ARE MOST SAFE TO OPERATE AND SHINE YOUR GOD-GIVEN COLORS FOR ALL THE WORLD TO SEE.**

Your path to your zone of genius may be muddy. Living in your zone of genius may be muddy, but it is where you are most safe to operate and shine your God-given colors for all the world to see. Knowing and embracing your zone of genius with joy gives a good

---

[16] Visit our ministry page at TKHornor.com

testimony and points others to our amazing and sovereign Creator God.

Living on the mud flats, out in the open, the very thing that makes the flamingo a target, is also his protection.

Embracing your genius may mean standing in mud. It may mean cold feet. It may leave you feeling exposed and vulnerable; but it also means protection, nourishment and giving glory to your Creator. You are never safer than when you are doing exactly what the Lord has called you to do.

To Consider:
Have you been delighting in or disdaining the muddy parts of your life and business?

Can you recognize this as part of God's perfect plan and thank him for it?

Do you know what your zone of genius is? If not, ask the Lord to reveal it to you. And if so, make some notes today about things you could delegate or even lay aside to allow you to live and act more confidently within that zone of genius doing exactly what you were created to do.

15. Nourishment From a Different Perspective

"Even the smallest amount of perspective can change how we are able to navigate hard times."
– Andy Andrews

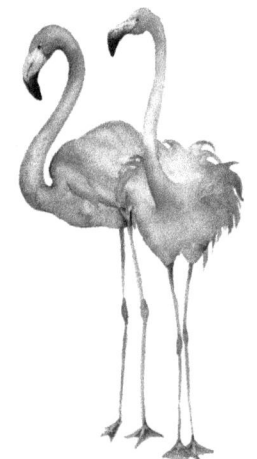

Flamingos will stomp in the mud and silt with their feet to stir up the crustaceans, mollusks, seeds, insects, various types of algae and diatoms. Then they lower their heads to the water's surface or even underwater to collect their food. They eat with their heads upside down using their mouth as a sieve to strain the water out while retaining their food.

This seems an almost dangerous design, especially given the fact that they are out in the open, very pink and obvious, and exposed to predators. But they rely on the protection of the group, as they're eating. Those with head upright can alert them to danger.

Sometimes, as Christians in business, what we judge as safe can be seen differently from a different perspective. It is for our own protection that we surround ourselves with others who can give us a different, and often nourishing or protecting perspective.

I think of Queen Esther who would have never left her safe position in the Queen's house to go before the King without a summons. She did something that seemed ridiculous and dangerous to those around her. She risked her life for her people due to the perspective of her wise old uncle that she may have been *"brought to the kingdom for just such a time as this."* And by doing so she saved a nation from annihilation (Esther 4:14).

Perspective: You may be just the one to do something about _____ (the issue God is pushing you to act upon).

I think of Mary and Martha, spinster sisters mourning the death of their brother and only provider, and their imminent life as beggars. Christ entered cheering their grief with

"Lazarus is dead. And I am glad for your sakes that I was not there, to the intent you may believe....Your brother will rise again....Said I not unto you, that, if you would believe, you should see the glory of God?" (John 11:1-46).

Perspective: I know how this looks, but remember God has a plan to show his glory through this circumstance.

And I think of Saul who was blinded by God to get his attention. And of Ananias who was asked to share with Saul the perspective that the God of the universe wanted his service. Each man originally saw the other as an enemy, but as they were willing to hear from God, God used each of them to change the other's perspective about God's people and God's work (Acts 9:1-18).

> **SOMETIMES WE GAIN THE BEST NOURISHMENT WHEN OUR VISION, PERSPECTIVE OR WORLD IS TURNED "UPSIDE DOWN."**

Sometimes you gain the best nourishment when your vision, perspective or world is turned "upside down." It's imperative for your own nourishment, growth and protection that you surround yourself with other like-minded "birds" who can help you filter information, news and even your own thoughts according to the wisdom and Word of God. Never be afraid to hear or look at things from a different perspective. In fact, I recommend that if you do not currently have a mastermind group who can offer outside perspective on your business, that you seek one out today! Refer to our list at KatieHornor.com/FLFresources.

To Consider:

How open are you to different perspectives? Do you pray or seek advice from trusted, mature Christians in business when you have decisions to make?

Are you teachable and able to filter things through the advice of trusted individuals? or are you choking on your own pride and insistent to go it alone?

Do you have a mastermind or group of like-minded people experienced in business who can ofter help or serve as a filter for the things you learn and the challenges you face as you grow your business?

If not, why not? Make some notes about what you would like to have in such a support group and begin to look for one.

Section 4
Prioritize Preening

16.
Work Your Gland

"Self-discipline begins with the mastery of your thoughts. If you don't control what you think, you can't control what you do."
– Napoleon Hill

It is estimated that a flamingo spends 30% of his day preening, cleaning his feathers, and oiling them with his oil gland. His feathers are his first line of defense from temperature changes, but he also uses them for swimming and flying. You might even say his feathers are the most fundamental thing to his success in life.

I have been blessed to participate in Jeff Walker's coaching program[17], and one of the advanced members is a former world champion martial artist. Ricardo[18] has told us that champions train a full month (8 hours a day, 5 days a week) out of every year on just the basic kick. They must master the fundamentals if they wish to compete as champions. He is always reminding us that in business we must also continually practice and master the fundamentals if we wish to emerge as champions.

One of the things I love about the virtuous woman in Proverbs 31 is that in addition to buying and selling and running a business, this lady focused on the fundamentals. She took care of her household first each day.

There have been whole books written about her, her business smarts and her wisdom so I'll not take time here. The point is that for success in your home, in your business, in your competitions, in your calling, you must give attention to the fundamentals. You must be consistently practicing and mastering the basics and taking care of the core things, or you put yourself and your business in danger.

At a particular time in our business when I was frustrated and nearly burnt out trying to keep all the things going, all the balls in

---

[17] Jeff Walker, ProductLaunchFormula.com

[18] Ricardo Teixeira, RicardoTeixeira.com

the air, I was gently reminded of Jesus' words to Martha in Luke 10:38-42... Jesus answered and said to her, "

Martha, Martha, you are careful and troubled about many things: But one thing is needful: and Mary has chosen that good part, which will not be taken away from her."

What stood out to me was the "one thing is needful". I know that Christ was speaking of sitting as his feet, learning of him, and fellowshipping with him, in the context of that story; but what I felt God asking me in that moment was, *Katie, What one thing is needful in your business right now?*

> **WHAT IS THE ONE THING THAT IF CAREFULLY OILED AND CARED FOR, PRACTICED OR MASTERED WOULD HAVE THE GREATEST IMPACT ON YOUR SUCCESS?**

What is the one thing that if carefully oiled and cared for, practiced or mastered would have the greatest impact on your success in doing what I've called you to do?

I now constantly come back to that question to guide my focus and plans for my day or my quarter. It's similar to the single focus question from chapter 9, but in an even more practical way:

- What one thing do I need to focus on first today?
- What one thing do I need to focus on next?
- What one thing do I need to learn, practice or master next?
- What one thing should be the main focus of my day so that I can be best prepared for success in what the Lord has placed before me to do?

To Consider:

If you evaluate all that is done in your business against the progress toward the long-term goal, you may find that only 20-30% of those activities actually push you closer to the goal.

What could you do to focus more effort or energy on that 20-30%?

Or maybe you find that most of what you do is busy work, not moving you toward the goal. In that case, what activities do you need to stop doing and what activities do you need to start doing to ensure that the goal is met?

17.
I'm Molting!

"What got you here won't get you there."
– Marshall Goldsmith

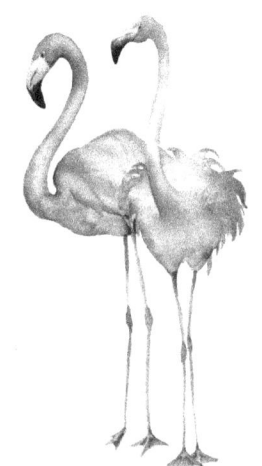

Flamingos shed and replace their body and wing feathers at very irregular intervals. This could happen twice a year or once every two years, depending on the particular bird's breeding cycle.[19]

As business owners there are also things that we may need to shed from time to time and I found it interesting that it also has to do with procreation.

---

[19] https://www.coolkidfacts.com/flamingo-facts-for-kids/

A healthy business is one in which you regularly evaluate your business: what's working, what's not, what tools you're using, how they're performing, which people work for you and whether or not their position, duties and work are pushing you closer to your goals in business.

At one time in our business I was managing 15 courses, 3 blogs, 9 websites, 12 Facebook pages, 13 Facebook groups and 13 Instagram accounts. I had several virtual assistants, subcontractors and about 15 different monthly tools running trying to keep it all together.

In one of our quarterly evaluations we realized that only about 40% of what we were doing was pushing us toward our goals. We then began the molting process to shed what was no longer beneficial.

As I am writing this, we have cut down to 3 course offerings, 1 blog, 5 websites, 6 Facebook pages, 7 Facebook groups, 3 subcontractors and one scheduling tool. And all of these are much more aligned with our long term goals. Giving up some of those sites was painful.

They were part of our story, part of what helped us get to where we are today. But we knew they were not part of the next chapter of our story. And we now have more time and energy to focus on growing the ones that are.

During that evaluation, we also realized that there were holes in our business. There were things and people we needed in positions to help us better grow in the direction of our goals, and now we were free to look for them.

I am not saying that you must downsize your business to be healthy, but I am saying that you must regularly evaluate all the parts and pieces to be sure they are helping you grow in the direction of your goals.

> **MOLTING IS NOT SHAMEFUL. IT'S A HEALTHY, NORMAL PART OF LIFE AND GROWTH.**

Pruning, purging (or in this case molting) is not shameful. It's a healthy, normal part of life and growth and it's a biblical principle. In John 15:1-2, Jesus said,

"I am the true vine, and my Father is the husbandman. Every branch in me that bears not fruit he takes away: and every branch that bears fruit, he prunes it, that it may bring forth more fruit."

In modern day business, molting or pruning may look like this:

Your goal is traffic: You may realize you've been busy in the content creation department, but what you need is to promote your content in order to grow. your traffic.

Your goal is revenue: You may realize that blog content is not helping you grow your revenues and that the money you're putting into writing may be better spent in promotion of your products while you refresh the content you have on a regular basis.

Your goal is list growth: You may realize that you can better grow your list by spending 30 minutes twice a week on networking activities to collaborate with others in your niche and share a lead magnet through that channel instead of (or in addition to) solely running ads to the lead magnet.

Just as flamingos regularly shed feathers in rhythm with their procreation schedule, your business will also need to regularly molt in order to continue on a healthy growth trajectory.

To Consider:
What activities, tools and expenses does your business need to shed in order to keep growing in the direction of your goals?

Are there things that you need to add to your business in order to keep growing in the right direction?

18.
What Black Feathers?

"Wise people are not always silent but they know when to be."

– Unknown

The flamingo has twelve principal flight feathers located on each wing. These black feathers are only visible when his wings are extended, which is normally just during the mating dance or during flight.[20]

These feathers could easily symbolize the importance of discernment in our lives. All of us have "black feathers." Feathers

---

[20] https://stinapabonaire.org/nature/flamingo-info/

that make us who we are just as much as the pretty pink ones, but may not be as pretty. You might say that they serve a purpose but do not need to be flaunted all the time. The flamingo only shows his black feathers on certain occasions, with a specific result in mind: mating or flying.

Christians in business need discernment to know when it's appropriate to show a black feather and when it's not. There is no need to flaunt the dark feathers in your life or business (or another person's) for all the world to see unless it serves a healthy and specific purpose.

> **THERE IS NO NEED TO FLAUNT THE DARK FEATHERS IN YOUR LIFE OR BUSINESS UNLESS IT SERVES A HEALTHY AND SPECIFIC PURPOSE.**

Ezekiel 44:23 says, and they {the judges} will teach my people the difference between the holy and profane, and cause them to discern between the unclean and the clean.

Proverbs 10:12 tells us that we should be swift to hear, slow to speak, slow to wrath {anger}.

Our business, *Handprint Legacy*,[21] is made up of two businesses: the Spanish language homeschool business and that of coaching Christian business owners and course creators. I have learned to go into conversations with new acquaintances asking questions first to see what they might need before sharing info about either of our businesses. If I go into it blurting out all that we do I may look egotistical, proud, or overwhelm them and never even find out what they do or how I might serve them.

This means that if that person needs our homeschool services, it may be months before they learn that we also do business coaching, or visa versa, but that's okay. In our love for them, putting their needs first and discovering how we could help them, you could say we used our feathers as intended.

This also means that a person asking my advice about the services of another business may not need to know of my bad experience (unless it was an ethical issue). There may be another way to caution them, if needed, than by casting doubt on that business' reputation.

Your "black feathers" may include both good and bad experiences that have shaped you.

---

[21] HandprintLegacy.com

As a non-business example, I don't need to tell every new acquaintance that I

- Played in my University's flute choir
- Sang on two music CDs produced by our Spanish church
- Directed an event for 250 people that won an award
- Was terribly hurt when abandoned by a high school friend
- Lost a baby through miscarriage
- Experienced the kind of postpartum depression that nearly drove me out of my mind
- Or that I struggle with auto-immune disease on a chronic basis.

Those experiences are important parts of my life, part of what makes me me, but they're not necessary or edifying to every conversation. It doesn't make me any less of who I am by not sharing, and it may be important *to share* those anecdotes with the appropriate people, but I use discernment to know if and when that knowledge or those experiences are relevant to the conversation—for the purpose of edifying.

Ephesians 4:29 says, Let no corrupt communication proceed out of your mouth, but that which is good to the use of edifying, that it may minister grace unto the hearers.

Yes, you have "black feathers." They're a part of you, part of God's amazing plan for your life; but it's not necessary, and may not even be God's design that you show them *all* the time.

To Consider:

Reread Ephesians 4:29.

Think about grace—unmerited favor, or divine enablement. Here's a good test for what to share when…

Ask yourself these 5 questions:
1. Is what I'm about to share going to be corrupt (evil, stinky, rotten, impure)?
2. Is it good?
3. Will it edify, build up, be positive for the hearer?
4. Will it add favor to this conversation?
5. Will this person walk away with an added ability or skill because I shared this information?

19.
Standing On One Leg

"What one piece of your business makes the most profit with the least effort? Do that over and over and over and over. Master it."
— Paul Jarvis

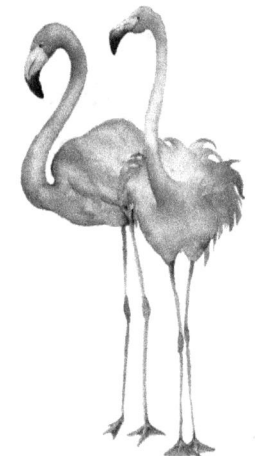

Have you ever looked at a picture of a flamingo and wondered how they can balance on one leg while sleeping? I mean, I can hardly stand on one leg when awake!

It is counterintuitive, because we typically view standing on one leg as being very difficult and we tend to equate difficult things with consuming more energy. But scientists have found that the flamingo actually uses less muscle strength when standing on one leg than two.[22]

They also believe that when in water, standing on one leg can help keep the flamingo's body temperature more stable.[23]

It turns out that though it doesn't look like it makes sense for the flamingo to stand on one leg when resting, it is the best way for him to conserve his resources.

There are things we can also do in our business to conserve our resources, though many times we don't see how these make sense without asking the Lord (or other trusted advisors), and sometimes the things he asks us to do don't make sense to those who are watching us either.

The Psalmist asked the Lord in Psalm 119:66, to teach {him} good judgment and knowledge.

And Scripture also says, if any of you lack wisdom, let him ask of God, that gives to all men liberally, and upbraides {reprimands} not; and it will be given him (James 1:5).

---

[22] https://www.discovermagazine.com/planet-earth/why-do-flamingos-stand-on-one-leg

[23] https://onlinelibrary.wiley.com/doi/abs/10.1002/zoo.20266

There is no need to stand on two legs in your business, using more energy or resources if you can stand on one and use less.

Here are some examples: you are using one tool for scheduling Pinterest and another for Instagram and a third for Facebook. Could you find a single tool that does all three and reduce that monthly expense? It would simplify logins too.

You have two people on your sales team, getting you about 20 clients per month. Could you still add 15 clients per month with only one sales person, spending less on salaries while increasing the profits and the attention given to each client?

You have an office that you pay rent for, but it's mainly only used for client meetings because your team are either remote or prefer to work from home. Could you also work from home, or from a coffee shop to be able to reinvest the rent money into the business or into the profit account?

You know you need to create 12 blog posts, 6 podcast episodes and 6 videos in the next 3 months. Instead of doing them one at a time as they become due to publish, could you batch produce all 6 podcasts in one day and pre-schedule them? Do the same for the other content. Often when I am not having to switch so often between tasks I find I can be more productive with my greatest resource: time.

You have a virtual assistant who is paid a high salary to do *all the things* you need her to do, including social media. Could you conserve some revenue and perhaps generate more by handing off the social media to an agency specializing in social for a monthly fee, allowing your assistant to replace those tasks with things that fall more in her zone of genius?

Or perhaps, like I did for several years, you spend 8 hours each month (+ 2 days recuperating) doing the financial accounting, reports and taxes for the business. I found that I could conserve my own energy, minimize stress levels and free up my time for higher earning activities by handing off those duties to a professional who can do it better and in less time.

We also found that we were promoting 10-15 different courses all the time, but after looking at the numbers we realized that 3 of them were bringing in the vast majority of the revenue. We decided to set aside those other 12 and focus on improving our promotion of those 3 to conserve resources and increase results, impact and profit.

> **CONSERVING RESOURCES DOESN'T ALWAYS JUST MEAN NOT SPENDING THEM, IT CAN ALSO MEAN USING THEM IN THE RIGHT WAYS OR SMARTER WAYS.**

Conserving resources doesn't always mean not spending them, it can also mean using them in the right ways or reallocating them in smarter ways.

To Consider:

Are there things in your business using up too much of your resources? Ask the Lord, (and perhaps your mastermind group or trusted advisor) for help in determining how you could manage things better for your business.

20.

When do you sleep?

"My candle burns at both ends;
It will not last the night;
But ah, my foes, and oh, my friends
It gives a lovely light!"
– Edna St. Vincent Millay

Flamingos are known to sleep both standing and sitting. There doesn't seem to be a preference. And since they'll stand on one leg when sleeping, they can even change legs without waking up. Some scientists believe this is because only part of their brain may rest at a time.[24] Perhaps this is to give the appearance of being awake and aware to would-be predators? We may never know.

---

[24] https://www.flamingos-world.com/flamingo-facts/

I believe entrepreneurs tend to have brains like flamingos; they never truly shut down. If you're at all like me (and I suspect you are) we're always thinking about business. The next project or opportunity is always on our mind. We look like we're "working" even we're supposed to be resting. Many of us are so well "balanced" that we can convince ourselves we're resting while to the rest of the world we still appear to be doing business as usual.

> **THE LORD CREATED US FOR WORK, AND HE CREATED REST FOR US.**

The Lord created us for work, and he created rest for us. We need rest. God himself rested on the seventh day after Creation as our example. In the Old Testament, we're commanded to rest on the Sabbath. Jesus, when on earth, rested. True, he did not refuse an opportunity to minister if it came on a rest day, but he was conscientious about regularly getting apart from the crowds to rest and to talk with the Father.

Frequently people tell me how impressed they are by all I get done, or all we do in our business. As an Enneagram type one, there was a time when I felt a pride in pushing myself to "burn the candle at both ends" as Edna St. Vincent Millay says. Do more, do more, do more, it gives more light... but when that light goes out?

When I first started cooking on a gas stove, it didn't take me long to learn that slow, low fire cooks the food and provides a meal for all to enjoy, while the brighter, hotter fire can burn things on the bottom while they're not quite done on top, and not fit to eat for anyone. Burning the food, or burning yourself out in your business, doesn't help anyone in the long term.

A flamingo who is not rested has no strength to fly, either in search of more food sources or in escape of danger.

Even so, a business owner who does not rest physically will not have the strength to continue searching for new clients, serving them, leading his flamboyance. He will not have strength to see and flee danger. Spiritually he will not have the strength to lead, make good decisions etc., unless he is also deliberately taking time to rest in the Lord and wait on his promises.

But they that wait upon {rest in} the Lord will renew their strength; they will mount up with wings as eagles; they will run, and not be weary; and they will walk, and not faint (Isaiah 40:31).

> **A SMART BUSINESS OWNER WILL REST WHEN AND WHERE YOU NEED IT. A WISE BUSINESS OWNER WILL PLAN IN REST WHETHER YOU THINK YOU NEED IT OR NOT!**

I've learned that rest is necessary to success and legacy. It allows for better focus, more concentrated effort and ultimately a healthier business and personal life. A smart business owner will rest when and where you need it. A wise business owner will plan in rest whether you think you need it or not!

To Consider:

Are you working all the time? Do you plan for rest in and from your business?

Are you taking time to rest in the Lord, and renew your strength by waiting on, trusting in, hoping in, resting in his Word and his promises on a regular basis?

What changes might you need to make in order for physical and spiritual rest to be a bigger priority?

Get the *Bible Study* guide for individuals & groups, or the *Faith Like Flamingos Journal* at FaithLikeFlamingos.com

CLAIM YOUR FREE AUDIO BOOK!

Forward the purchase receipt of this book to

FLF@katiehornor.com to get the audio book FREE!

Section 5
Think Pink!

21.
That's Using Your Legs!

"The only thing more dangerous than ignorance is arrogance."
- Albert Einstein

The flamingo has only one line of defense and that is their very powerful legs. If they become aware of the predator soon enough they will be able to fly away. It's beautifully fascinating to see them rise up, flap their wings and begin to run with their webbed feet on the water's surface, gaining speed with their long-legged strides and then rising into the air as they take off in flight.

Flamingos aren't great fighters, but they know that. Their legs were built for wading and running not for fighting, so they must be vigilant of the dangers and have a plan for escape.

2 Timothy 2:15 tells us to *rightly use* the Word of Truth, and in the following verses he goes on to warn us to
- Shun profane babbling (godless chatter)
- Depart from iniquity (sin)
- Flee youthful lusts
- And avoid foolish questions just meant to start arguments.

Verses 24-25 say: the servant of the Lord must not strive; but be gentle unto all men, apt to teach, patient, in meekness instructing those that oppose themselves...

I often wonder how many Christians in business have missed the correct use of our "flamingo legs" by misunderstanding these teachings?

I invite you to ask yourself: having been given the gifts of strength and knowledge how often do I stand in place, arrogant, ready (and sometimes wanting) to fight and defend myself, when God says to flee the danger?

I know I am often likely to post on social media "because I haven't posted today" instead of because I have something purposeful and valuable to give my followers. Could that be considered babbling?

Have you, like me, been secretly tempted to enjoy the competition's apparent failures, smirk when someone is the brunt of a funny joke (disregarding their feelings) or lust after the followers, reach, or revenues of some other business?

Do you use *foul* language (see what I did there?) or do you post something controversial on your social media or blog because you know it will stir up an argument, get a reaction or gain publicity? Is that motivated by a pure heart?

"All is fair in love and marketing" they say, but is it? Each of these are examples of delaying obedience, playing with the things Scripture says we should be leaving behind us.

Things that will make the Christian stand out in the marketplace are his opposition to strife, his refusal to engage in petty arguments for publicity sake, his ability to pursue peace, his gentleness to all races and classes of people, and his ability to teach patiently and with meekness.

One of my business coaching clients had to choose how to use her legs recently when one of her clients got involved in the dark arts.

Instead of pridefully standing and thinking *"I can handle this. I can still work for her without approving of her work or getting involved in it,"* Jennifer chose to run away, to discontinue working with her and look for clients elsewhere, honoring her gut, her company values and God's Word. In the end, God brought along a new client whose work was much more in alignment with her values and also paid better. [25]

To Consider:
Knowing God's Truth is key to knowing what to flee in your business and when. Are you regularly studying God's Word to know him and what he wants of you?

Do you let pride tell you "you can handle things"? Or do you run from the dangers like the ones mentioned above? If you don't protect your business and the people you lead, who will?

---

[25] Jennifer Elia: jennniferanneelia.com

22.
Migrate Regularly

"Only those who risk going too far can possibly find out how far one can go."
– T. S. Elliot

Flamingos migrate when the weather becomes too chilly or when the food sources dwindle and they go in search of other food. In a year they may migrate between two or three main areas in search of food.

As business owners you're not searching for food, but you are in search of new clients, customers and people to impact with your message.

It reminds me of the "Great Commission" passage in Scripture: Go therefore, and teach all nations, baptizing them in the name of the Father, and of the Son, and of the Holy Ghost: Teaching them to observe all things that I have commanded you: and, lo, I am with you always, even unto the end of the world. Amen (Matthew 28:19-20).

And while your message, product or service is not *the Gospel*, you can give the Gospel right along with it. As a Christian in business, you can teach them of Christ as you teach them your skill or expertise. Your actions will often do more to teach them of Christ than your words will.

And just as it is with the Gospel, we must go find these people, not expect that they will come in search of us. Some will. That's true; but the majority of your clients will come to you because you stepped out in search of the people who need your message.

Going to find them may look like joining forums or Facebook groups online to find your people. It may mean attending live events, business fairs or other gatherings where your people are likely to be.[26] It may mean pitching your story to magazines, other blogs, podcasts, YouTube channels, TV networks, press, live stages and media outlets.

---

[26] Mega list of business events: BloggingSuccessfully.com/conferences

In 2019, I spoke on 18 stages sharing our story. Then, in the three months before this book was published, I set a goal to share our story with 180 podcast hosts. (Perhaps you learned of this book through one of those guest episodes.)

It was scary. I didn't know how many would want to have me on the show, but I knew I had to *go* in search of my people.

It's uncomfortable, yes. It may feel risky moving into new territory. And hey, no one said flying was easy for the flamingo… But the more you do it, the more you find you can do.

> **YOU MUST BE REGULARLY SEEKING OUT THOSE YOU CAN SERVE, OR YOUR BUSINESS AND MESSAGE WILL BECOME EXTINCT.**

Most of those I reached out to were wonderfully kind, and I have had coaching clients, mastermind clients and joint venture partners find me because I put myself out there as a guest on a podcast. Others found me in an internet search for "business coach," they heard me speak at a conference or read my bio on a guest post I wrote for someone else's site.

"If you build it they will come" is one of the greatest myths in business. You must be pro-actively migrating around in search of your food (i.e. client) sources. You must be regularly seeking out those you can serve, or your business and message will become extinct.

To Consider:

What are you doing to search out new clients? How much effort are you putting into serving the ones you have, so they will tell their friends?

Ask the Lord for wisdom on where to begin reaching out and how to best put yourself out there as the solution they are looking for. Make a list of the ideas he brings to mind and start taking action today.

23.
Pink Weather Ahead

"Your life does not get better by chance, it gets better by change."
   - Unknown

Flamingos can detect rain from a distance. On the parched coast of Nambia, flamingos appear to know when the rains are due in the usually dry area that lies 500km away. *"How?"* you ask, *"It's too far away to see lightning or hear thunder."* You're right. And those who study the birds in this habitat think it's possible that flamingos are sensitive to the minuscule drops in barometric pressure that signal oncoming rainfall. [27]

---

[27] https://www.discoverwildlife.com/animal-facts/birds/facts-about-flamingo/

As I'm writing this, my family and I have just celebrated our ninth anniversary of living in Campeche, Mexico, on the Gulf Coast. In those short years, my body has become extremely sensitive to the changes in barometric pressure here at sea level.

During half of the year we almost never experience rain. When the rainy season starts, however, I can tell when it will rain because of the pressure in my head or the heavy lethargic feelings in my physical body even before we see the rain clouds form. If I'm not paying attention to the signs though, I may not realize why I feel that way until the rain starts. Then it all makes sense.

In Deuteronomy 28: 1-14, God pronounced a string of blessings over his people including that of good treasure, blessings upon their work, and rain:

The Lord will open unto you his good treasure, the heaven to give the rain unto your land in his season, and to bless all the work of your hand: and you will lend unto many nations, and you will not borrow. And the Lord will make you the head, and not the tail; and you will be above only, and you will not be beneath; if that you hearken to the commandments of the Lord your God, which I command you this day, to observe and to do them: And you will not go aside from any of the words which I command you this day, to the right hand, or to the left, to go after other gods to serve them (vs 12-14).

They were assured his blessings would come if they obeyed his commands.

In the world of business, the rules are always changing. Things today are not what they were when we started in 2011 and 2012. And things ten years from now will not be as they are today.

Think about this…
- In 1879, Edison invented the electric light bulb.
- In 1985, Marconi invented the radio.
- In 1927, the first television was invented.
- In 1953, the first automated mobile phone system for vehicles was launched.
- In 1973, the first call was made from a handheld mobile telephone device.
- Prior to 1983 the internet did not exist.
- Facebook and the podcast were invented in 2004.
- Twitter was invented in 2006.
- The first iPhone released in 2007.
- Pinterest was invented in 2008, but was still by invitation only as late as 2011.
- Instagram was invented in 2010.
- Amazon's Alexa and the Periscope live video streaming app were invented in 2015.

In 2006, it was a luxury for your business to have a website. A mere 14 years later it is a liability for your business not to have one.

> **CHRISTIANS IN BUSINESS MUST REMAIN CONSCIOUSLY AWARE OF AND ADAPT TO THE CHANGES IN THE ATMOSPHERE OF BUSINESS AND THE WORLD AT LARGE.**

Just as flamingos, and sometimes humans, can sense a change in the weather, Christians in business must remain consciously aware of and adapt to the changes in the atmosphere of business and the world at large.

I believe that if we want to see good treasure and blessing upon our work, we must keep up to date with changes in policies and governing laws and with advances in technology, communication, marketing and customer service. We must embrace each in as much as they will help us further obey God's commands, his calling on our life and his purpose for our business.

Why? Not just for the blessing he promised in Deuteronomy, but also so that others will see your work and glorify the Father.

Let your light so shine before men, that they may see your good works, and glorify your Father which is in heaven (Matthew 5:16).

Whether therefore you eat, or drink, or whatsoever you do, do all to the glory of God (1 Corinthians 10:31).

It's important though that we not fear the future. The flamingo doesn't fear the rainstorm. He runs to it because he knows the changing pressure brings rain and that means nutrients and food and blessing. We must not fear the changes and new pressures that bring change. Our God was and is and is to be almighty (Revelation 4:8). He is with us always (Matthew 28:20). He holds us in his hand (John 10:27-30). We have nothing to fear, rather when we keep up to date with the changes we are in a better position to serve our people.

To Consider:

Are you taking steps to keep up to date with the changes in the business world? Do your business and website give a good testimony to potential customers and clients? Does your work, website, or customer support appear "behind the times?" Are you using the modern tools available to serve your people better, or are you afraid of changing seasons and exploring new things?

Ask the Lord to give you an awareness of change, but not a fear of it, and wisdom to know how to embrace it to serve your people better while giving glory to him.

24.
Pink Forever

"Everybody wants loyalty, consistency, somebody who won't quit. But everybody forgets that to get that person, you have to be that person."
- Unknown

Flamingos are fiercely loyal, to their mates, to their babies, to their flamboyance. They stick together, they travel together, they return to each other if they have to separate in search of food.

The flamingo's loyalty reminds me of a friend of ours who is a college sports fan. It doesn't matter that they didn't play on the team or even attend most of the games in person while they were in school, they still cheer for them every season. Winners or underdogs, playoffs or not, this guy and his house and car and children and dog all proudly wear the colors and emblems of "his team"—all the time. I'm sure you're thinking of someone like this right now. Nothing you could do could convince him that his team is less than the best. He is fiercely loyal.

God's faithfulness to us is like that. He said in Hebrews, *"I will never leave you or forsake you"* (13:5), and later we read that Jesus is the same, yesterday, today and forever (13:8).

It doesn't matter what we do or say, where we go, or what may be done to us, God loves us fiercely, loyally. And that love will never change.

For I am persuaded, that neither death, nor life, nor angels, nor principalities, nor powers, nor things present, nor things to come, nor height, nor depth, nor any other creature, will be able to separate us from the love of God, which is in Christ Jesus our Lord (Romans 8:35-39).

As a Christian in business, how do you love your people? Your family, yes, but *your people*? How do you love the ones God has placed in your flamboyance: mastermind, network, focus group, coaching group, membership etc.? How do you love your share holders, business partners, customers, clients, followers, and audience?

Are you loyal? Do you love them as Christ loves? Maybe you *think* you do, but do *they* think you do? Is your love obvious to them and to random observers?

> **JUST AS SOMEONE CAN BE ALL FIERCELY LOYAL TO THEIR FAVORITE SPORTS TEAM, YOU CAN BE FIERCELY LOYAL TO THOSE YOU WORK WITH AND FOR.**

Just as someone can be all fiercely loyal to their favorite sports team, you can be fiercely loyal to those you work with and for. It's a choice to go all crazy fan-girly over them.

My grandmother once told me, "

Katie, your main job as a wife is to be your husband's biggest fan. Always make him look good to others. Always speak well of him, never evil. He's not perfect, but they don't need to know that. Cheer him up, cheer him on. Brag on him. Let him have no doubt of your love and loyalty."

I've found that the same applies in business. We need to be *our peoples'* biggest fan. Get excited for their wins, cheer them on when they're down, speak good of them always. Never let them doubt that you believe in them. It's a choice to love. It's a choice to be loyal. You have the power to choose. And as Jeff Henderson says,

"When you're for the people in and around your business, the people in and around your business become for you."[28]

To Consider:

Are your people loyal to you? If not, why not? What could you do to encourage loyalty within your flamboyance? Are you loyal to your people? Write out some ways you could *show* loyalty to your …

- Family
- Share holders
- Business partners
- Network/mastermind group
- Clients/customers
- Followers

Therefore all things whatsoever you would that men should do to you, you do even so to them: for this is the law and the prophets (Matthew 7:12).

---

[28] *Know What You're FOR* by Jeff Henderson, 2019, Zondervan

25.
Don't Fear the Plastic

"You don't need to compete when you know who you are."
- Bernadette Jiwa

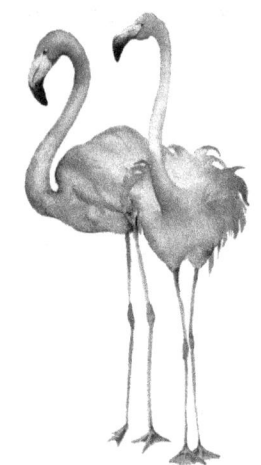

Don Featherstone of Massachusetts invented the pink plastic lawn flamingo, which has been gracing lawns since 1957. (Yes, though it is a bit ironic, I believe Featherstone is his true last name.)

The "official" pink flamingo is from Union Products, though the patents and official molds for the classic lawn birds have been transferred to different companies through the years. Plastic birds are still in production today and, believe it or not, there are actually more plastic flamingos in America than real ones.²⁹ Madison, Wisconsin, a city in one of the northernmost US states, even named the flamingo as their official City Bird!³⁰

In Romans chapter 14, Paul talks about comparing ourselves and our work to that of others. If you have time, stop here and read the whole chapter, but listen to these verses specifically:

For it is written, as I live, says the Lord, every knee will bow to me, and every tongue will confess to God. So then every one of us will give account of himself to God (vs. 11-12).

Let not then your good be evil spoken of (vs 16).

Let us therefore follow after the things which make for peace, and things wherewith one may edify another (vs. 19).

We tend to think of a plastic flamingo as an imitation, an imposter or a fake. They are prevalent and famous in their own way but they don't hold a candle to any of the "real birds." And if you ever seen a live flamingo parade in front of a plastic lawn ornament, you'll notice that he's neither impressed nor intimidated. He doesn't cower. He walks tall. He doesn't attack it, talk to it or engage it in any way. It is simply not a threat.

---

[29] https://www.thespruce.com/fun-facts-about-flamingos-385519

[30] https://madison.com/wsj/news/local/govt_and_politics/city_hall/city-designates-plastic-pink-flamingo-as-official-city-bird/article_e4c74006-905e-5c82-ad11-1ee368c900fc.html

There are competitors, antagonists and imposters in life and in business. You will encounter at some time or another others who try to look like you, look better than you, impersonate you, steal attention from you, criticize you unjustly or intimidate you.

Your God is bigger. Have faith. Stand tall. Confidently show your faith in God's master design for you, your life, and your business. Don't let a "plastic flamingo" discourage you from being *who you are*, and doing what *you* were created and called to do.

> **DON'T LET A PLASTIC FLAMINGO DISCOURAGE YOU FROM BEING WHO YOU ARE, AND DOING WHAT YOU WERE CREATED AND CALLED TO DO.**

James 2:17-18 says, even so faith, if it has not works, is dead, being alone. Yes, a man may say, you have faith, and I have works: show me your faith without your works, and I will show you my faith by my works.

Walk tall, my friend. Be bold. Be loyal. Be pink. Be *you*. Live out your faith in your calling displaying your calm confidence that God created you just the way he wants you to be, so that in life and in business, others will see you and your works and glorify the Father which is in heaven.

To Consider:

Do you have a fear of man that keeps you from living out your faith in your life and business? Ask God to replace that fear with a confidence in his perfect love that casts out fear (1 John 4:18).

Do you find certain people or situations intimidating? Create a plan now for how you will respond the next time to show a confidence in who and whose you are instead of the normal fearful reaction.

How can you continue to walk tall, be unique and fulfill your purpose in bold color? Make a list of the ways you will apply what you've learned in this study to your life and business and set a date on your calendar for 3 months from now to come back and review this list and what you've learned here.

Note from Katie:
You are amazing! I am so proud of you for finishing this book. It is my prayer that God's grace (divine enablement and unmerited favor) and peace will be multiplied to you through knowing him, and through the knowledge of Jesus our Lord, according as his divine power has given to us all things that pertain to life and godliness, through the knowledge of him who has called us to glory and virtue (2 Peter 1:2-3). May you continue to confidently show your faith in bold color, like the flamingo, in <u>all</u> you do for his glory.

~Katie

Thank you for reading my book!

Note from Katie:

I really appreciate all of your feedback, and I love hearing what you have to say. I need your input to make the next edition of this book better.

Please leave me a helpful review on Amazon or on social media using the hashtag #FaithLikeFlamingos.

Share your selfie with the book on Instagram sharing your favorite lesson from the book. Use the hashtag #FaithLikeFlamingos as I will be surprising a few of our readers with a special gift.

Thank you so much!

- Katie

Find the *Faith Like Flamingos Bible Study* guide for individuals & groups, or the *Faith Like Flamingos Journal* on Amazon or at FaithLikeFlamingos.com

Forward your receipt for purchase of this book to FLF@katiehornor.com to get the audio book FREE!

www.ingramcontent.com/pod-product-compliance
Lightning Source LLC
Chambersburg PA
CBHW071501080526
44587CB00014B/2181